VANISHED FACES

Odile Suganas

PUBLISHING
NEW YORK♦JERUSALEM♦LONDON

Vanished Faces
Published by Devora Publishing Company
Text Copyright © 2010 Odile Suganas

Appeared in Lithuanian under the title *Atminties Mozaika;* published in 2007.

Previously published in French as *Mosaique: ou reconstitution d'une mémoire* by GRAPHEIN, Paris, France

Translation by Solange Solomon,
Revised by Catherine Porter

COVER DESIGN: Benjie Herskowitz
TYPESETTING: Daniella Barak
EDITORIAL AND PRODUCTION DIRECTOR: Daniella Barak
EDITOR: Sara Rosenbaum

All rights reserved. No part of this book may be used or reproduced or transmitted in any form or by any means, electronic or mechanical, including photocopying, recording, or by any information storage and retrieval system, without written permission from the publisher.

Soft Cover ISBN: 978-1-934440-90-2

E-mail: publisher@devorapublishing.com
Web Site: www.devorapublishing.com

Distributed by:

Urim Publications
POB 52287
Jerusalem 91521, Israel
Tel: 02.679.7633
Fax: 02.679.7634
urim_pub@netvision.net.il

Lambda Publishers, Inc.
527 Empire Blvd.
Brooklyn, NY 11225, USA
Tel: 718.972.5449
Fax: 781.972.6307
mh@ejudaica.com

www.UrimPublications.com

First edition. Printed in Israel

To Father, "Master of the Castle,"
and
To Mother, Die Scheine, who has joined him.

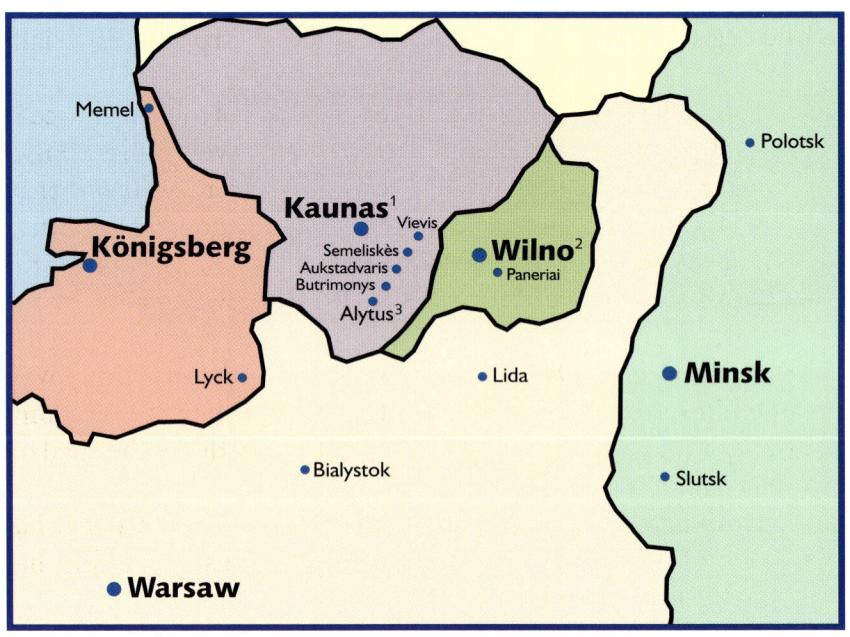

Interwar Map

[1] Lithuanian name for Kovno, as was called between the wars.
[2] Polish name for Vilna, as was called between the wars.
[3] Yiddish name is Alyte

Foreword

The beginning of the new century is full of surprises, especially for the survivors of Nazi camps.

Not only has what is called "the *Shoah*" found a special place in intellectual pursuits, instigating historical and even philosophical works, but some heads of state once decided to meet in order to work together toward the development of a pedagogical project.

Their meeting took place on January 27, 2000, the date of the 55th anniversary of the liberation of the Auschwitz camp by the Red Army.

On that day in 1945, only a few people – sick or lying low – remained in the camp. The 60,000 others, from the various camps in the Auschwitz complex, had already been sent down the road on what has come to be called the "death march."

This march has often been recalled. I do not know if it has been celebrated in song or recreated in drawings, but a film has been made about the subject.

I was part of it for nearly three days. The SS fired their guns at random. A great many of those who attempted to escape were killed because the SS, wild with fury at the wretched souls who were hindering them in their own flight, kept right on killing, far from the gas chambers.

A few managed to run away. I was one of them.

Odile Suganas's moving book reminded me of all that.
I had the feeling I was witnessing a "death march" in reverse.

Foreword

To be sure, no threat was hanging over the author, except that of reliving, in her mind, the tragic episode symbolized by the Nazi death factories.

In fact, the Nazi hell is not what Odile Suganas was looking for. She was after the faded images of *Vanished Faces* that still lived in her memory.

As she set out to piece the past together, she was going to discover a remote world and bring it back, little by little, one face at a time.

The grandmother is the symbol of it all. She plays a part in the reconstitution of a past that fascinates, yet seems ever more remote, even beyond reach.

A name, Vilnius, now Vilna, arises from memory. Vilna, the historic capital of Lithuania, of a country where Judaism was particularly creative. Great religious thinkers lived there; the Bund – the Jewish socialist party – was born there; historians, writers, painters, many remarkable creators drew their inspiration there.

Odile Suganas, who nourishes her recollections with surviving photographs, set out to search for a past that is gone forever.

She refers to a vision passed on to her by her father, who had been familiar with the vast horizons that she would revive through imagination.

Her father's death opened up a new chapter in her life. She decided to go looking for the world she had rebuilt from scraps of memories gathered from one person, then another.

The pilgrimage starts in Vienna, a town that does not belong to any of her recollections but where she can find echoes of Strauss, Mahler, Mozart...

What did people expect to find there, besides evocative songs recalling a *Gemütlichkeit*, a warm feeling that seems to remain alive only in memory?

Next comes Berlin: an odd itinerary, one might say. The Berlin where the Wall has collapsed, a Berlin where people sing and dance.

But another Berlin comes back to mind, the capital of "the ponderous old Germany, without a conscience. The weight of History." We begin to realize that the road to the East is taking shape.

A plane is about to take off for Vilnius, her Vilnè. What is she going to find there? "A land that is yours forever, yours because your loved ones lie there."

These words drift through the air in the middle of the forests.

Over there, in the cemetery, her grandmother is waiting for her.

But there is a town for her to discover. Does she find it similar to the one she carries in memory, the one she has imagined?

At an antique dealer's, she finds Sabbath candlesticks.

But she is drawn toward the cemetery, for there she will rediscover – with the help of memory – the world she has always considered her own. It is "the realm of the sleeping dead." They will not wake up. Still, kneeling in silence, she speaks to her grandmother: "Here I am. Never have I been so close to you."

And other faces come back to her mind: her mother; her aunt Dora, a medical student; David, a writer, who was "liquidated" …

Episodes belonging both to tragedy and to history seem to spring back to life. The author's evocations take us to Minsk, to Smolensk, and then still farther away, to Kirghizstan, to Uzbekistan.

On that road, we discover her uncle Benjamin, who enlisted in the Soviet Army and was wounded during the battle between Koursk and Orel, which lead to the Stalingrad victory.

Odile Suganas invites us to go along with her on a quest for a world that only recollection can bring back to life.

Vilna is no doubt the central point. But the quest for the past knows no frontiers.

We are now transplanted to Israel. Odile unearths a portrait of her grandmother painted by Moshe Rosenthalis, and visits the artist's studio. Her way of describing the paintings she finds there reveals her familiarity with art, obviously an important reference point in her life.

But Odile's quest is insatiable. Along with her, we discover other villages, other landscapes. Through her talent, she gives life to characters which seem familiar to us.

Some episodes might easily become plots for a novel. But Odile does not simply imagine. In the course of her discoveries, she recreates spaces for the living from what had become places reserved for the dead...

On one occasion, at Semeliskes, I think, she finds a small plaque mentioning the murdered Jews.

We are now in Kaunas, once Kovno, where her uncle used to live.

An observation confirmed by all those who, like her, have set out in search of a past still alive within them: "No more fragrant smells, no more bustling streets, no more caftans. Nothing looks as it used to."

But there is a Jewish museum, improvised inside a small, green dacha.

We meet a series of people in the search for someone who may have known one of her uncles, a respected writer, David Umru, the last director of the Jewish theatre in Vilna. He was arrested and deported along with five hundred other members of the Jewish intelligentsia.

This uncle becomes the leading figure in her quest. Many people knew him, and Odile meets several witnesses to his career.

We follow her as she rediscovers an outstanding personality and creative artist (he painted and created theatre scenery; his talent was acknowledged outside Lithuania).

Foreword

A visit to Ponar cannot be avoided. Here, in this resort on the outskirts of Vilna, in the heart of a magnificent forest, seventy thousand Jews were put to death...

You set out in search of recollections, looking for signs of life, and you find memorials to the dead. And all of a sudden, a statement springs up, exuding pent-up bitterness in a poetical outburst: "Birds have no borders; nothing – and everything – belongs to them."

Will Odile return to Vilna? Of course she will! It is the resting place of her grandparents.

And now Odile is looking back upon her own past when, as a child in hiding, she was given a home by Marie and Gaston Lacave. She lived there in Mirande, in the Gers region, for three years.

This time, Odile starts from her own recollections. We are now in a different universe, a world "dug up" by her father, a world to which they owe their escape from zealous French policemen.

This other world is closer to us. Odile shared the "adventure" with hundreds and hundreds of Jewish children who were given homes by good people – homes and "hide-outs" (as they were called then) that enabled them to survive.

The Lacave family is about to receive the award of Righteous Among the Nations granted by The Holocaust Martyrs' and Heroes' Remembrance Authority of Yad Vashem. The ceremony is one of those extraordinary moments when past and present merge, calling up a period during which History was being written, the History now being revived long after the fact.

On the Lacave parents' graves. She has reached the end of her journey. A journey that has taken us back more than fifty years ago.

But after accompanying Odile on her quest for the past, for the shadows of her relatives – a quest, really, for herself – we realize that it will never come to an end.

She cannot yet fully appreciate the impact her discoveries may come to have as time goes on.

Without claiming prophetic gifts, we understand that, from now on, Odile will no longer set out in search of a past that is over,

Foreword

but in quest of a world that has resumed its place in her memory. The shadows have recovered their faces.

The reader who has followed her throughout her journey has shared her discoveries and her feelings. But feelings are not enough to piece the past together. One needs a gift for storytelling – and this, Odile Suganas has.

Once, when I was in Moscow for a conference, my hosts learned that I had been born in Lithuania, and suggested that I make a quick visit. Much to their surprise, I turned down their offer. I was too young when I left my native country; I was convinced I would find no trace of anyone in my family there.

In the album my parents left me, there are grandparents' faces, faces of parents with their children, faces of people I never knew, because I was too young when I left. I did not want to go back to a land of shadows.

But Odile Suganas has made the journey, and when I read her account of it, I felt that I was reliving something we had in common. I think that all her readers, including those who bear in mind other journeys, other landscapes less filled with the tragedy recalled here, will take part in this pilgrimage, one that is full of feeling, but that, thanks to the last chapter, leaves us with a glimmer of hope.

Henry Bulawko
President of the Society of the Deportees of Auschwitz
and of the Camps of Upper Silesia

The Journey

My journey to Eastern Europe was made in very small steps. Unconsciously, inexorably, I had been preparing for it. The quest had begun in my early childhood. Nothing particularly spectacular about it – slow advances with long pauses wherein nothing much happened.

Once, when I was a little girl, I had been accompanying my parents to my elementary school during the election, when someone leaned toward me and asked, "How about you? Who would you vote for, if you could?"

Very shyly, I muttered, "For Grandmother." I do not remember anything but the long silence that followed.

That was my first call eastward. Life went on.

Grandmother was an entity unknown to me. A family, a country, a memory I would sense, she remained an enigma. Grandmother was a kind of wall – impossible to reach, forbidden – that had haunted and oppressed me all my life. Why couldn't I see her? I would imagine an Iron Curtain, slightly rusty, pulled down between her and the rest of us – my parents and me.

Very little was said about her at home. Letters came regularly from Vilna; Mother sent parcels there to help her get by. I remember the recurring phrase "a letter from Grandmother." Mother used to be on the lookout for suitable items – neither too luxurious nor too ordinary – so they might get through the customs censorship unnoticed. It took a lot of know-how and loving care. During these preparations, Mother kept a long, silent conversation going.

As an adolescent, leafing through a photo album, I discovered, among other people, my uncle David. He was young and handsome, with a lion's mane. A gifted painter and writer, he made a living as a professional photographer. I took his photo up to the attic, where I had a place of my own.

The author's uncle, David, known as Umru.

And then, one day, when I was twenty, I heard a loud scream in the house. It was Mother.

She had just received a letter from Vilna, not from Grandmother this time, but from Uncle Benjamin.

Grandmother had passed away some weeks before.

Afterward came a blank, and total darkness. I don't know; I no longer remember.

This half-century of suffering is, for some people, unspeakable and forever buried in their hearts and souls as in a profound abyss.

So it was for my father.

I began to age when my father was hospitalized. Day after day I watched him.

He was sailing away.

Time was suspended. Sitting facing me, he would say, very calmly, "I don't want to die." His beautiful blue eyes would shine. Sometimes, facing the hill, he would say, "You mustn't cry when I'm not here anymore. Can you see my 'castle' up there?" By "castle," he meant the grave where he would lie. Was he getting used to the idea of dying? No, it wasn't that. It was his placid humor, dropping as a stone would fall into sleeping waters. He had known sweeping vistas that I had never seen, but that I could discover in my imagination. Without them, it was hard for him to live. They were images of his homeland, to which he was bound because he had been born there – a land where he had known hunger and fear, where he had struggled, and where he had also experienced moments of happiness. He could not forget his youth; it was imprinted on him to the core. It was not with a light heart that he had left his homeland, his *Lite*, his Shtetl by the lake, with the horses, the forests, and the tales about wolves.

The years carved a noble beauty in him; he grew more and more handsome. His features became more stately, his gaze, magnificent. His gestures grew

The author's father, Albert Suganas (1901-1985), two years before his death.

Vievis Lake

more majestic, slower and more acute. He had found his inner voice and harmony. He did not speak much. Whenever he did, what he said was accurate and thoughtful. People listened to him. He was a contemplative man, in love with nature. His search for beauty led him to seek elegance and delicacy. A generous man, he did not know how to turn down a request.

Money is "secondary," he once said to an acquaintance of mine. "We must forget it as soon as we have a little."
He loved music and animals. He was compassionate, strong, and vulnerable. I loved to comb his undulating, silky white hair. He was happy to let me do so.

In his later years, I used to catch him humming a Yiddish tune, and sometimes he would get up and try a dancing step – the kind Chagall would have appreciated.

As I joined in, we were happy together, sharing the fragility of the present moment. Whenever he wanted to be precise, he quoted proverbs or phrases in Yiddish, Russian, or Polish. He translated them to me, using circumlocution, but his words lacked the concision, the intense flavor of the original tongue.

My father carried in himself a country, an inner wound. His life had been hard work, which he had loved, and which prevented him from thinking too much about the past – except, perhaps, in his dreams. Sleep was his refuge, his rejuvenation.

It was dawn when he died.

During the days just before, the sun had spread "manna" over the town, a golden hue mixed with touches of pink that made those days both sweeter and crueler. When I approached his "castle," his "estate," I was surprised to feel proud that he was the lord of this land.

Birds have no borders; nothing – and everything – belongs to them.

After my father passed away, my inner world began to collapse and my journey to Eastern Europe commenced.

Vievis, 1922, in front of the Suganas family home. Standing, left to right: Albert Suganas, age 21; his niece, Rosy Chahan, visiting; Rachel Suganas, his youngest sister; his nephew, Chimele, son of Meier Kurgan, who is seated at the far left.

It began in Vienna.

Why did I go there? For its culture, for Strauss and Mahler, for the Habsburg Empire, and also for Freud and Mozart.

The plane landed in a heavy rain. It was autumn already and I appreciated this weather; an appropriate welcome. I then remembered that once, at wintersports, I had met a pleasant, lively woman. Born in Vienna, she had managed to flee the country in 1938. She was nineteen years old then; it was just before the Anschluss. In Austria, anti-Semitism was raging. She harbored such distaste, such loathing for that place, that when I told her that I wanted to go there, she could not understand it. She described the spirit of denunciation that used to prevail, the hate and humiliation that Jews were subjected to there.

Still, she went back regularly to look after the family tombs.

I wandered about the streets of Vienna, its avenues and alleys, from the Parliament to St. Stephen's Cathedral, from Mozart's house to the Capuchin crypt. I rode the great ferris wheel at the Prater, I thought of *The Third Man*, I scrutinized Viennese faces and tried to figure out why…in the hope of reading a change. But I only perceived, sadly, an air of slightly provincial elegance, and unparalleled conservatism.

Arriving in front of the imposing building at 19 Berggasse, I went through the archway and up the splendid staircase to ring the doorbell, as if on a private visit. The flat was somewhat empty of furniture and seemed to exude a certain sadness. In the hall, a walking-stick was still waiting for its owner, and a hat was hanging on the wooden coat rack. There was a sofa in place, but the one Freud had actually used was in London.

The only visitor, I was greeted by the woman in charge of the Museum, and we chatted. The names in the visitors' book mostly belonged to foreigners. "Very few Austrians ever come here," she said.

She told me a little about her life. A German Jew, she had lost everything; the sole survivor in her family, she felt better and

The opening scene of the film "The Third Man" takes place in front of the Pallavicini Palace, where the protagonist claims to live.

more useful here, with her job keeping her busy, than out in the larger world, now turned upside-down, where she had too many memories. She shuttled between Vienna and Germany. The visit took a warmer, more personal turn, for I was familiar with such too-often-heard stories.

As the mistress of the house, she commented on some of the items displayed, most of them replicas. We arranged to meet again that evening in a Viennese cafe, along with two of her friends. They even proposed to me a meeting with Sir Simon Wiesenthal, survivor of extermination camps who devoted his life to tracking down nazi war criminals; but I declined the offer, unwilling to disturb this busy man, especially since I would not have time to sufficiently prepare for such a meeting, as I was leaving Vienna for Salzburg the day after.

I was happy to be able to talk and ask questions in a trusting atmosphere, with people who knew the city and Austria.

I walked so much in Vienna that I went home limping, convinced that I had a bone spur on my left heel.

I visited superb museums, admired the paintings Hitler had intended to appropriate, enjoyed Schönbrunn for its intimacy and charm, all of this intermingled with operas, *Bratwurst*, *Käselkuche*, and *Sacher Torte*.

And then I took the bus to go to the Jewish cemetery. Once there, I walked through the tidy Catholic churchyard, with its perfectly aligned tombstones; it struck me as tasteless and academic, *ohne seele* – bereft of soul.

Inside the old Jewish cemetery in Vienna.

As if suddenly plunged into an enveloping warmth, I lost myself in the old Jewish graveyard. A waiting world, asleep from time immemorial.

Thick trees protected this hidden world where the silence had a special quality, echoing the past, where the bushes skillfully encroached upon the tombstones, clasping them in a russet embrace. The leaves fell one by one, like drops of crystal; occasionally, a bird flew overhead, mute, while another whistled a plaintive cry.

Alive, I greeted the souls in the deserted alleys. The world of yesteryear was resting there, an illustrious past lost and gone forever. Here lay the glory of an Austrian society, eradicated for all time.

I wandered through the alleys, bowing before these unknown dead.

November 9, 1989: the fall of the Wall.

Sitting in front of the television screen, my mother and I watch the event. "Well done," she says, and I agree.

Astonishing and unexpected...Berlin, bewildered, sings and dances.

I telephone a friend who was born in Berlin to tell her that we share her joy.

Before I set foot there, it used to be Berlin the thunderbolt, Berlin the somber, Berlin the tragic. A dark cloud, flashes of

The Berlin Wall on Bernauerstrasse. This is the place where construction began, which created an unbearable, illogical situation, causing drama and traumatic experiences that affected the population. For example, cutting a building in two, where one side was suddenly on the east and the other side was on the west.

lightning; a world apart, full of anguish and fear; an atonement, an explosion. The shock of Berlin. Kennedy's Berlin. Poverty-stricken Berlin – from superabundance to indigence.

The world is changing, reaching the tipping point, becoming a different world. From gloom to madness. Everything is happening fast, too fast. Berlin! Marlène,[1] where are you? Where is the ponderous, old Germany, without a conscience? The weight of History. It was irresistible; I was drawn to the East. I had to go to Berlin – *Nach Berlin* – without a flag, without a banner, without vengefulness or anger. To see. To ascend towards the East. To transcend the block in my heart.

---

1 *Marlène Dietrich, born December 27, 1901, was a German actress and singer. She became famous in the 1930 film,* Der blau Angel, *and then continued her career in the States, eventually becoming a citizen. She strongly rejected the hitlerian regime and went on tour during WWII singing for soldiers all around the world to help raise morale. She died in Paris on May 6, 1992.*

We are all the Berliners of some dictatorship or other; we must liberate ourselves. Berlin, the ephemeral center of a defeated Mittel Europa, of crushed and choked nationalities.

Birds have no borders; nothing – and everything – belongs to them.

I am impressed when I set foot in Berlin. I am "with" and "in" History, in a monumental, reunified city.

I am drawn toward the Brandenburg Gate. That is what I want to see first. I realize it is rather small…it is also close to the gloomy, amputated Reichstag – a witness, pregnant with meaning.

Everything in Berlin is KOLOSSAL. It is not a beautiful city, but a megalopolis, strewn with green patches in the spring weather, with trees in full bloom; this is what redeems the western part of the city. Berlin – a shelter for artists and political militants – lived on a reputation that lasted only twenty years, at the beginning of the century.

The wall has been pulled down, but large sections still stand. It remains an entity, and it will linger in people's memories. The East Side Gallery, kept to bear witness, still bears signs of protest, torches calling out for peace and forgiveness. Cemeteries from before and after.

I am moved. My eyes take in those gigantic, dancing frescoes, shouting the horror of subservience, and the roaring, gaudy colors in geometric planes, clamoring the stupidity of totalitarianism. What a breathtaking homage to the memory of the past and of a future that has now become the present…

Berlin, May 1991. On the left, the Wall in the distance; in front of it and to the right, a no-man's-land where a freight car has been turned into a temporary café.

The original Wall in the former Jewish quarter.

But minds are damaged, sick from a mental and physical imprisonment that will not soon heal. So sing out, colors, dance away, spirits, and on another day like November 9, 1989, we shall once again shout out another victory.

I wander through a city where everything is contrast, and the more I wander the better I understand the gap that separates East from West.

From East to West I go. I could make good use of Wim Wender's wings.

I walk along Bernauerstrasse, where the wall was built. In front of some of the parts that remain, as if in protest, a screen of bushes and birch trees has sprung up, with its green foliage shining in the sun, defying the scrap-heap – the concrete structures splitting the seams of a no man's land. A wall, a rupture, with inscriptions: "Why?" "Liberty!" "A unified world!" "No more war!" "No more wall!" Never again *nach Berlin*, but *wie Berlin*.

Unter den Linden is no more. *Kaput*. A kaput that has given way to ponderous, lifeless official buildings. And I walk. I pass Aeroflot and see that flights are leaving for Paris, New York, Vilnius.

"Vilnius," the capital of Lithuania, departure 15:10, arrival 18:45, 500 Deutsch Marks. It's all there. And I look at the board, at that line: 15:10 – 18:45, 500 Deutsch Marks. I stare at the board; it opens an old wound, an unappeased dream.

Vilnius – to me, Vilna – further north and east. A three-hour flight... A family lived there once, with a story of its own. Father, you were born there, and you died somewhere in Europe, in the west, much further south, in the green Normandy land that is yours forever, yours because your loved ones lie there. In Vilna, on the Baltic, many of my loved ones rest tragically. They wander through the air amid the forests, and I wish we could assuage our grief so that we might meet at last.

I claim a right of ownership over any piece of land where my deceased ancestors lie. There are lands that are mine, a few square yards in cemeteries or in unknown sites, in various places in old Europe where my forefathers have fought for them. All of us have the right to meditate on the soil that is nourished by the blood of our blood; no one can keep me from going to bow before their tombstones.

The moment has come.

It is a radiant, warm day. The sky, a pastel blue, is pure and serene. Everything seems so easy, so normal, that I can hardly believe that I am about to be in Vilnè, as said in Yiddish, to me.
Sitting by the window, I am well aware that I am approaching Lithuania. I discover the very first trees, the very first harvests, and can barely wait to breathe in this whole land, take it all in, catch up with lost time, move from anticipation to fulfillment.

Speechless.

Seen from the sky, Lithuania is a puzzle of little mirror-like lakes and patchy green forests. An annunciation.
Soon. The plane is about to land – it is landing... I nod goodbye to the flight attendant. She doesn't know that I am descending into the reality of my dream.
The Vilna airport has a pleasant, provincial aspect. So do the beardless, somewhat awkward, young soldiers who stamp our passports. I look beyond the small crowd of people grouped together, waiting for someone who belongs to them. I look around in the hope of a familiar face, knowing it is impossible. I feel sad.

Grandmother is resting in the cemetery over there. She is waiting for me.

In the car that takes me to town, the narrow avenue opposite the airport offers me its first trees, with their soft green leaves waving in the sun between shadow and light.
On the alert, I am interested in everything.

My hotel is on the edge of the Neris river. When I open my bedroom door, I am confronted with the 1950s: dark, heavy furniture, outdated wallpaper, massive, square lamps, an antiquated bathroom... I am steeped in a dismal exoticism that leaves me unruffled.

No telephone. Cut off from one world so I can be more fully imbued with another... But I shall realize soon enough that I can't do without modernity.

Anything can happen.

I go out.

The heat seems to have driven away all the pedestrians. Only the trees are there, glimmering – a relief from the invisible, impassible, overpowering heat. I meet people who do not suspect a thing. The avenue looks beautiful with its thick trees. There are no longer any of that kind in western Europe.
I arrive on a large square where I find a huge, ugly temple: it is the cathedral. Once I have crossed the square, I head toward Pilies street in search of something. I walk into the silent inner courtyards. I keep on walking. Everything is quiet and peaceful. Too peaceful. Could it be a ghost town? I don't know what to think. I have just arrived and was expecting a shock. No fragrance, no shouts, and the passers-by I meet remain silent.

I turn into an alley and spot an antique dealer's sign. Inside the shop, I discover two Shabbat candlesticks that were identical, except in size, to those Mother brought with her to France sixty years ago. The same embossed grapevine, framed with its leaves, its clusters fanning out in the same tripod shape. I continue strolling at random through the old city, where renovations are under way in some streets, have been completed in others. The architecture reflects the many strata left by the city's countless invaders – a memory of history.

I am drawn to the cemetery. I won't find it that first day, however; not until the following day, near Ukmerge Avenue, lost in the midst of a complex of roads, hidden behind a factory. An anachronism.

An inner courtyard in Vilnius. It has an exquisite charm, thanks to the clairs-obscurs prism perspective on the trees.

I push open the gate. A hedge of white hawthorns, standing guard, accompanies me into the realm of the sleeping that is "yours forever, yours because your loved ones lie there, dead." I continue walking down the main alley, a photo in hand. It is the one of my grandparents' grave taken by Uncle Benjamin before he left Lithuania for Israel in 1969.

The tombstones of the author's maternal grandparents: on the left, Stesia Liackovitch, 1887-1960; on the right, Zalman Liackovitch, 1878-1931.

There they are. Grandmother is at rest in the shade of large branches. I look at the marble tombstones, soiled by time; set on two cement blocks, surrounded by five other smaller ones; connected by iron bars, turned rusty by bad weather. In the center, I see a large square space, overrun by moldy moss and dead leaves. I meet my grandparents at last.

Kneeling in silence, I say to my grandmother, "Here I am. Never have I been so close to you." And the palm of my hand goes from my heart to the Hebraic inscriptions. We have finally found one another, protected from the uproars of the world, in the silence of our torments.

I have reached one of my goals.

I think of Mother, and of her sister Dora, who was in the Vilna Ghetto and ended up at Treblinka – the youngest, who was studying medicine in Vilna – exterminated – and of her brother, David, known as Umru – exterminated.

I had the grave restored, and I went back with a bunch of arum lilies and white roses.

After the war, when Grandmother came back from Tashkent, she lived on Komanoru Street, now Jaksto Street. Two of her children survived the war: Benjamin – seriously wounded between Kursk and Orel – and Liuba, my mother.

On Sunday, June 22, 1941, at four o'clock in the morning, Alyte, now Alytus, was bombed. There were many casualties. Leaving everything behind, Benjamin and Grandmother set out for Minsk. As Minsk was also under fire, they made their way toward Smolensk. There, in freight cars, they were relocated to Frunze, in Kirghiztan, where they stayed only a short time: residency permits were hard to get.

Tashkent, in Uzbekistan, marked the end of their journey. Benjamin worked in a cooperative. In the early summer of 1942, he joined the 16th Lithuanian National Division as a volunteer and fought in the front, between Koursk and Orel, as part of the 5th unit of the 167th regiment. The battles were fierce and deadly. That is when the Germans started to pull back. Benjamin was seriously wounded, almost killed. It was the augur of the capital turn, of the long dreadful victorious battle of Stalingrad, that foretold the German defeat.

Benjamin found out later that a German soldier, hidden in the wheat fields, not far away, had shot him in the temple. As luck would have it, he was in motion at that very moment.

Advancing in files of five, the soldiers in his unit would move forward and throw themselves on the ground. The first soldier in Benjamin's line was killed at once. Benjamin, the second soldier in the group, then became the first.

Instead of killing him outright, the bullet passed through his jaw, and after being moved from one hospital to another, he was eventually sent, by night, in a medical train, to Leningrad – the only place where there were specialists capable of attending to his wounds.

I am holding a photo in which Grandmother is on a balcony that I believe looks out onto Jaksto Street. I am looking for the street. Nothing. I walk through the maze of buildings, and I am able to identify the right one thanks to the wrought iron designs. I walk across heaps of earth and look at the ancient acacias overhanging the balcony where she used to think of us, so far away, and yet so near.

To be where she used to live gives me the impression of being in a sanctuary. I look at everything so as to miss nothing. Impatience and the will to see and to know bring tears to my eyes. I pause for

Odile Suganas

Stesia Liackovitch on her balcony (Vilna, Komanoru Street, 1949).

a long moment in order to contemplate this particular sight. Her presence is the only thing missing – there, on the balcony, waiting for me, waving her hand at me.

It is a beautiful, yellow brick building, probably dating from the thirties. I walk through the entrance. Inside, an elegant staircase, although slightly dilapidated. I walk up the stairs, heart beating, to the top floor. Once on the landing, I feel stage fright, but I knock. Not a sound; no one answers. I remain there in suspense, then walk toward the door, opposite. Someone comes. I do my best to explain who I am. I am invited to step into the apartment.

In the spacious room sits a large stove. Did they remember her? What was she like? I would like so much to see her as she appeared to these strangers – her neighbors.

They have nothing to tell me. Most of the time, she would stay on the balcony and would not go out much. They remembered only

Stesia Liackovtich lived in the left-most apartment on the top floor, where two French windows can be seen behind the balcony.

the younger generation: Benjamin, his wife, their children. There is nothing more to add. I can't stay any longer. They would not understand. Unsatisfied, I reluctantly take my leave.

Before leaving Lithuania, I went back and sat on a stone to look once more at the apartment and the balcony, and I cried softly. At that very moment, I had the feeling I was leaving Grandmother for good. I anchor deep inside me this landscape, testimony to her life.

Some time later, continuing my peregrination and my research in Israel, I discovered my grandmother in an art book dedicated to the work of Moshe Rosenthalis. I had never forgotten what Mother told me a long time ago: "A portrait was made in Vilna and is now in Israel; where, I don't know." I felt an ache, knowing that she existed somewhere. I had buried this information deep within.

My way to the East was not yet traced. Nor was the reconstruction of the mosaic. Grandmother was escaping me once again.

I felt helpless.

In the painter's workshop, a few steps separate me from the room where I am going to discover and meet...her. Shyly, I go on in. I turn around, and there *she* is, right behind me – arms folded, head tilted to the side, looking down, weary.

I step forward, then back, the better to take it all in: A beautiful face illuminated by deep blue eyes expressing the strain of living, quiet and stoic. Fine whitish gray hair gives great gentleness to the dark brown tonality of the portrait. The features of the face are hollowed out by shadows and light. A strong presence; a profound sadness.

My maternal great-grandfather, Hirsch Wolf Meierovitch, used to live in Butrimonys,² where I have an appointment with Riva Bogomolnaja-Lazanski, a native Jewish woman, a survivor of the massacres. She had been in hiding with her sister in the forest; together they joined the underground.

The village is deserted, the weather endlessly beautiful.

Photos in hand, I look closely at the dainty, colorful houses, imagining what life used to be like, and on the lookout for my great-grandfather's home. It cannot be this one or that one because, from what Mother used to say, it used to be large and beautiful.

The author's mother, Liuba Suganas, between her two aunts: Sonia on the left, Haye on the right.

---

2 *Baltrimantz or Butrymance are alternate spellings; Butrimantz in Yiddish*

Hirsch Wolf Meierovitch, a wealthy grain merchant, owned land and at one time even a mill.

Each celebration was the occasion for a party to which the whole village would be invited. Mother always told me how happy she was to go to Butrimonys on holidays; for her, it remained the image of happiness and a peaceful place where she would once again see her grandfather and remember how her aunt Sonia used to pamper her there. After Sonia got married to a man from Vievis and became Sonia Jacob Katz, the pampering had to wait until Mother visited her there. To Butrimonys, Mother would ride with a cousin in a horse-drawn carriage or,

Four generations appear in this photo, taken in Butrimonys in the summer of 1936. In the center, Odile's great-grandfather, Hirsch Wolf Meierovitch, holds his great-granddaughter, Solange Suganas; on the left, his granddaughter, Liuba Suganas, holds her son, Wolf Louis Suganas, on her lap; on the right, his daughter, Liuba's mother, Stesia Liackovitch.

in winter, in a sleigh. She enjoyed the sound of the bells hanging from the horse's harness.

After my great-grandmother died, my great-grandfather married a townswoman who had nothing of the *baleboste*, the housewife, about her. They had a daughter, Genia, who was also pampered.

All these details are whirling in my head. Where is my great-grandfather's house? I go back to the square, where Riva Bogomolnaja-Lazanski soon joins me.

She is short, and her straight, gray, shoulder-length hair is held by a barrette. She is wearing socks and flat-heeled shoes, holding a cane in one hand, a shopping bag in the other.

Her head tilted, she looks straight at me with pale-blue eyes. She is not young, nor is she very old. I show her the photos. She is overcome by a wave of emotion. She knew each person in them. She knew my great-grandfather. She lived across the street from her friend Genia; they went to school together. She burst into tears, then becomes voluble. The sky suddenly darkens, thunder roars, gusts of wind come up one after another, the weather turns wild. She cries.

Tension and emotion rise and a heavy rain falls on us. We seek shelter and she continues to tell me the story, my story, my family's story. My great-grandfather's excessive generosity, the parties, his second wife, and Genia for whom she used to sew, who was a poor student at school, raised like a "lady" – Dverele, *die gringele*, little Dora, the skinny one.

She recalls how my great-grandfather, after having lost his entire fortune, sold everything he had left, went to synagogue, put his tallit on his head, buried his face in his hands, and sobbed. She recalls how, in the mid-1930s, he went to live in Wysoki Dwor (now Aukstadvaris), where he was exterminated along with his entire family during World War II. She also remembers Mother, *die Scheine*, the beautiful one. She goes on and on... Time unfolds, emotion is at its height. She kisses the photos.

"Where is my great-grandfather's house?"

"Here, very close by, and his lands are across the street. His house was pulled down not too long ago, and another one was built in its place."

Raindrops trickle down the window panes. The storm is over. We continue talking. She tells me more about Genia.

Following the changes in my great-grandfather's financial situation, Genia went to live in Alytus, with my grandparents, to earn her living. She disappeared at the very beginning of the invasion of the Nazis somewhere between Alytus and Wisoki Dwor, where her parents lived.

A horse-drawn carriage passes by.

The rain has stopped, but the menacing black and gray sky resembles a Delacroix painting. We are walking toward my great-grandfather's house, at least where it used to be.

Horsecart passing by on the street where Hirsch Wolf Meierovitch used to live.

Slowly, too slowly. Only the earth, the trees, the spirit of the time bear witness to an era when *als iz gewesen*, "everything has been" – those are Riva's exact words.

"Here it is," Riva says.

A large, expensive-looking house, with bricks that make it look modern, stands on the site. Motionless, I try to imagine the big house Mother used to talk about, and I wish I could see her as a child, with her long hair, on a visit to her grandfather.

The slate has been wiped clean, the past forever wiped out.

We walk on to the cemetery. Riva is silent. She has relieved, for a moment, a world gone by.

Standing out against the sky, we see a hilly space surrounded by a railing. Sparse, tall trees stand guard. Supple high grasses invade the grounds sprinkled with white flowers. Everything seems indelible, frozen for all time. The blue of the sky and the white-streaked green of the landscape display a dichotomy of life and death in which I can scarcely believe. Nature coddles and crowns the dead with its royal covering. Will I find an ancestral trace here?

Most of the tombstones have disappeared. Stolen. Some are lying around in chaos. Many are buried amid grass, wildflowers, and moss. For a long time, we bend over, seeking out a family name – but in vain. Riva offers comments on one family or another, but nothing about the family Meierovitch. Vanished in the storm.

Mother was born in Alytus; that is where we are going. I have the address of her house. I know it was bombed on June 22, 1941. Still, to see the street where she had lived happily with her parents, brothers, and sister is of paramount importance to me. I need to breathe the air they breathed, tread the ground they walked on. Mother has mentioned the Niemen river, the Russian bank on which they used to live, opposite the Polish bank. I have also heard the story about the Cossack who came to court her as he played the balalaika.

We are now on Juozapavicius Street. It looks more like an avenue than a street; its oldest part is lined with trees. A local resident's good will notwithstanding, I am unsuccessful in my search for witnesses. The name Liackovitch rings no bells.

We stop in front of a stately synagogue made of yellow brick, closed, under repair. There are only seven Jews left in Alytus.

We walk toward the surrounding woods where sixty thousand Jews were massacred. In each spot where death occurred, a white cube has been erected. There are many cubes.

Since Lithuania gained its independence, some truths have been exposed. The Soviets had concealed the liquidation of the Jews, turning the killing ground into a battleground where Soviet citizens had fought bravely, heroically. This is what Riva tells us. It is confirmed by the Lithuanians who have come along with us.

Father was born in Ievie, now Vievis: a small village on the shore of a lake, surrounded by a forest of fir trees; a resort from the beginning of the twentieth century; fashionable, owing to its healthy climate.

The road from Vilna to Vievis is very beautiful. Forests and lakes everywhere. The church is my landmark. Before I left for Lithuania, Mother told me that Father's house had been behind the church, on the lakeshore. So we walk to the stone church. With its two towers, it looks like a citadel surrounded by a small protective wall. We walk through the streets where the brightly colored wooden houses are surrounded by attractive gardens in which flowers are growing, vying with each other in the form of beauty – lilacs, arum lilies, lupins, and the famous poppies that Mother mentioned so often. There they are, looking fresh despite the hot sun.

When we inquire, we are told that a Jewish woman and her son are living in the village. We walk to their house. After we have

explained why we have come, we are warmly received, but we do not get any more information; the mother, an elderly woman, settled here only after the war. She tells us how she survived through massacres, tortures, and persecutions, and then sought refuge in the forest with the underground. All of us are in tears.

We walk along the lake, which offers the idyllic landscape of a peaceful

Lithuania, June 1926: Albert Suganas as a soldier, age 25.

On the way to Vievis.

resort. I think of Father. I have in front of me the concrete proof of what he always loved: water, nature, and open space. There is also a small figure with a cap on his head, sitting in a boat that looks like a nutshell, holding his oars, awkward as a duck in his efforts to row away from the shore.

Photos in hand, we continue to look for the family home in the village streets. Much to my regret, none of the houses appears to be my father's. The villagers say that before World War II, most of them belonged to the Jews. The name Suganas, or Shugan, means nothing to them. I wish father were still alive to be here with me. I meet an old peasant woman and ask her the same question. But she can't help me. So I ask her where the cemetery is.

"You won't find it. Impossible." But then she takes us there.

Vievis: a view of the church from a window in the house where Albert Suganas was born.

The garden in back of the Suganas family home. Odile is standing near the door. The church towers can be seen at the far right.

Two or three miles outside of Vievis, she has us stop on the highway, along an embankment. It is impossible to imagine that there is a cemetery near here, as we walk into a forest of oak, birch, and acacia. The ground is studded with huge lilies of the valley. I have never seen anything so beautiful. But in the midst of this wild garden, broken tombstones have fallen beside the graves they once marked; vaults, gaping holes, have been vandalized and looted. I notice that the tombstones have been desecrated recently. The old woman protests that she is not responsible, it is not her fault.

"Those who are responsible," she replies, "are the Soviets; it was when they built the highway, in the sixties."

But the excavations are recent. Silence. No one looks at anyone. The young Lithuanian woman who has come along furtively wipes her eyes.

Vievis, 1922. Top left: Salomon Suganas, one of Albert's older brothers. Top right: Hermann Suganas/Chahan, Albert's oldest brother; in front of him, his daughter, Rosy. Middle row, right: Samoie Samelov, Hermann's father-in-law; left, the author's paternal grandfather, Wolf Suganas. Bottom right, Marie Samelov, Hermann's mother-in-law; left, Hodle Suganas, the author's paternal grandmother.

I stop in front of an intact tombstone, lying beside its grave. The Hebraic inscription says:

*Abba Isaac, son of David Jacob Katz.
We shall always mourn at your grave;
we shall always regret that we could not see you grow up.
You were taken from us at the end of your second year,
on the day of Roch'Hodech Kislev 5687 (1927).
May his soul be united with the community of the living.*

The tombstone of Odile's second cousin, Abba Isaac Katz.

I have found my second cousin's tomb, Aunt Sonia's son – the aunt Mother was so fond of, the one she used to visit at Butrimonys.

I called Mother the following morning. She told me that the child had died suddenly while playing in his room. He was two years old and left a twin brother. I thought to myself that it was better that way: he was spared extermination.

We are driving toward Semilishok, now Semeliskes. Massacres for which Lithuanians were responsible took place there. Many members of my family had sought refuge there, thinking they were safe. Salomon Suganas's wife, Tsine, was born there.

(Above) Vievis, 1923. Standing, upper left, Albert Suganas; center, his brother Salomon; far right, Olga Suganas, his aunt. Seated, left to right: Albert's brother-in-law, Meier Kurgan; Albert's brother, Hermann Suganas/Chahan; Meier's wife, Hiene Kurgan; a sister of Albert Suganas.

(Right) Vilna, 1906. Odile's paternal great-grandfather, Hessel Shugan. (Courtesy of Zev Rosen, U.S.A.)

The forest in Semeliskes where the massacre took place.

The little country road opens onto a tapestry of wildflowers.

We have to find the forest path leading to the site. When we arrive, silence broods over thick, tall, dark trees. We, too, keep silent. A small sign mentions the massacres.

A railing surrounds a large rectangular plot. Some of the wild grasses have been cut down. We walk toward the monument with its inscription in Hebrew.

Kaunas (Kovno) is the town where my uncle Umru lived and worked. His book *Javer* (Rust) was published here in 1937 as well as his other known book, *Derner* (Thornbushes), in 1939. The blue-and-white synagogue is spacious. We are greeted by a small group of men who welcome us and invite us to go up to the balcony where women usually sit.

It is now Sunday. Life has slowed down; people wander idly about the streets. I have the impression of going back in time; the atmosphere is old-fashioned. A girl in her white, organdy, first communion dress is walking with an older sister and a younger brother. The solemnity of the occasion has given her a serious look, accentuated by her metal-rimmed glasses and the halo of white flowers crowning her fair hair.

I am looking for Umru's publishing house, number seventy-six Laisves Aleja (Liberty Avenue), where twin rows of trees offer the passers-by their thick canopy of leaves. The building stands before me, the color of rosewood, with two balconies.

I look at the mailboxes. The publishing house no longer exists. It was more than fifty years ago…

I am waiting for Lazare-Elie Aron, a member of the local Jewish community. He is going to take me around Old Vilna to show me where large and small ghettos used to be.

He is a tall, slender man with a slight stoop and a sharp expression in his pale-blue eyes.

His Yiddish is trenchant. I can hear in it the same energy as in Uncle Benjamin's speech. He offers a running commentary on the old city, pointing out a small plaque erected at the entrance to the old ghetto where the Judenrat once stood. The narrow alleys of the ghetto have been destroyed and replaced by German Street. It is a wide street and without a guide, it would be impossible to get one's bearings. Nothing remains of the past, although by looking closely it may be possible to spot the location of an oratory marked by the star of David. Lazare-Elie shows me one.

No more fragrant smells, no more animated street life, no more caftans. Lazare-Elie often stops in front of a stately building and says, "This used to be the home of the So-and-Sos; they were very well-to-do. The X family lived here, the Ys over there. Here is a plaque commemorating Antokolski. The Hebrew high school stood here, the library there, the main synagogue over here." Nothing of the past remains. Everything has been emptied out; everything has been swept away.

He points out the French Embassy, one of the most beautiful buildings in Vilna, where General Koutouzov had his headquarters during the Napoleonic campaign. The university is close by. We sit down opposite the church. Lazare-Elie seems sad. Later, I realize that he was exhausted. This strong-willed man does not tell me that he is seriously ill. He is reliving the Vilna of former days. I am very lucky to have met him.

He shows me the streets that have kept the names they used to have in what was once "the Jerusalem of Lithuania": Gaon Street, Jews' Street, Glazer street, and Antokolski Street. (A few weeks later, in the real Jerusalem, I was happy to be reminded of this and to discover more about Vilna – streets, landscapes, atmosphere – in an art exhibition at Yad Vashem, the place of memory, featuring Jewish painters of the Baltic, especially works by Nahum Alpert, Alexander Bogen, David Labkowski, Esther Lourié, Jacob Lipchitz, and many others. I still had more to learn about Baltic Judaism...)

Vilnius, June 1992: Lazare-Elie Aron (1918-1993).

The following morning, I find Fania Brantsovsky in the lobby of my Vilna hotel – a survivor of the Vilna Ghetto. A small woman in socks and sandals, skirt and blouse. She shows me where she was hidden during the Nazi occupation, before she joined the underground.

We go next to the new Jewish museum, set up somewhat informally after independence in a small, green *datcha* near Gediminas Avenue.

In the room where photos are exhibited, on the right wall, I recognize David. Fania is staring at me as if he had come back to life.

The caption, in Yiddish, reads:

The streets of the old town in Vilnius. Its arches, once much lower, were raised by the Soviets.

> *Dod Umru, a young writer from Kovno, author of* Derner, *a book of short stories. He was a writer and editor of the newspaper* Vilner Emes. *In 1940, he was named director of the Jewish State Theatre in Vilna. He was arrested by the Gestapo[3] in July 1941 and was later declared missing.*

So he had not been entirely forgotten.

I have an appointment with the elegant wife of a Lithuanian general, Tsila Jiburkiene. I tell her that I have discovered my uncle David's photo in the Jewish museum.

---

3   "Gestapo" is what is written in the museum's caption, but in fact it was the Lithuanian collaborators, Ipatingas, who arrested Umru.

David Liackovitch, known as David Umru, age 20.

"David who?"
"Liackovitch."
Silence.
"His pen name was Umru."
"Umru! Umru! You are Umru's niece! But I used to know him well! I never missed his lectures, none of my friends did either, we were all in love with him."

And, acting on a shared impulse, we fall into one another's arms. We are linked by a bond out of the past. Arm in arm, we walk along like old friends. I ask, "What was he like? What was his outlook on life?" I want her to keep talking, to tell me everything…

"I didn't know him personally, I was too young… He was handsome, intelligent…" As she conjures up the past, her face brightened; she must have been remembering happy days from her youth.

Als iz gewesen, Riva had said. A cruel truth.

Today I have an appoint-ment with Yacub Josade, a writer who surely knew Umru, or so have I been told.

He lives on the ground floor of a house that has seen better days. Everything in his apartment dates from the 1930s. The shelves overflow with books, paintings, and sculptures; the desk is littered with files; the desk lamp, the chandelier, everything here would warm an antique dealer's heart.

"Yes, indeed," he says, he knew Umru very well. He asks me what magazine I work for.

"I'm his niece."

His expression becomes serious, and his interest keener.

In slow, clear Yiddish, he begins to speak.

"I saw him for the last time in June 1941, at a first

Vilnius, 1992, the writer, Yacub Yosade (1911-1995) in his apartment.

night at the theatre. I never missed his openings. He was the director of the Jewish Theatre in Vilna. I was living then in Kovno. I went back to Vilna in July, and the first thing I asked when I got there was, 'Where's David?' He had been taken away along with five hundred

The Liackovitch family. From left to right: top, David (Umru), Dora, Liuba; middle, Stesia and Zalman (parents); bottom, Benjamin.

Left to right: David Liackovitch; David's wife, Liuba Liackovitch; Liuba Suganas holding her daughter, Solange Suganas; Dora Liackovitch; Benjamin Liackovitch holding his nephew, Wolf Louis Suganas, on his shoulders; the author's grandmother, Stesia Liackovitch; the author's great-aunt, Genia Meierovitch.

other members of the Jewish intelligentsia. At that time, only men were being arrested. He had tried to escape with his wife and baby, but the Germans were everywhere. They had to return... He was separated from his wife and child and taken to the Lukiskiu prison. No one got out of there alive.

"They lived in a flat on Šubaciaus Street, not far from the Philharmonic. I remember a tiny baby, probably just a few days old.

"We had gotten acquainted in Kovno in 1935. Umru belonged to a Zionist organization. He wanted to leave for Palestine. But then he became a Communist and turned against Zionism. His position was difficult, since ninety percent of the Jews were Zionists then. He and I organized the Jung Vilna and Jung Kovno movements with Haim Yelin, the Poetess Leye Rudniski, and the poet Hirsch Ocherovitch. We worked together to produce a literary magazine.

"He was very good-looking, not very tall, with thick hair. A brilliant man, as good a speaker as he was a tactician, in the good sense of the word. He was very subtle, a good friend, warm and open, *sehr interessant*, yet his writing and his literature were still harsh, uncompromising, categorical...

"He worked in Kovno as bursar in a sanatorium to earn his living. He was a man of character. He neither smoked nor drank. We got on very well together. He had a sense of humor, which he never used to hurt others, unlike me – I was virulent. In that sense, we complemented one another.

"It was not by chance that he chose the pen name Umru. Umru means 'anxiety,' 'restlessness,' 'agitation' in the political sense. He chose the name because it corresponded to his idea of militancy. He wanted things to change."

He showed me an anthology of literature, *Kalendarz-Literacko Historyczny*, published in Warsaw in 1966 by Jacob Gutkowitz, in which David was featured and where his first book, *Javer*, was mentioned. "Born in 1910 in Alytus, killed in Vilno in July 1941 by the Gestapo."

He added, "He was very calm. We were completely different. I liked to show off; he didn't."

I asked him if he had any of Umru's poems, books, or articles. He answered that among his many books and manuscripts he had some of Umru's texts, but he did not feel up to looking for them at the moment. He promised to send copies of whatever he could find.

He had a fainting spell during the course of our interview. He was often unwell. We both waited patiently until he felt better.

The next day, some Lithuanian friends took me to the Lukiskiu prison, a cluster of dismal, grayish-yellow buildings that included a church. Here he must have contemplated his impending death, with his wife and baby in his thoughts.

Anguish and horror brought an end to a life full of promise.

The following day, at the Book Palace, the journalist Eliohu Seif told me more about David.

He had met him in Kovno just after completing his secondary studies, in 1938 or 1939. As a young student, he was impressed by Umru, to whom he looked up as a sort

Vilnius: the Lukiskiu prison, still in use.

of glamorous older brother. Once, seeking advice, he went to see him at the newspaper where Umru worked. The writer was at his desk, sketching stage sets. Greatly surprised, Seif wondered how anyone could do so many things at once.

"Writing didn't bring in enough money; to earn his living, he worked in a sanatorium. At the time, Umru was also the editor of the *Yiddishe Zeitung* in Kovno, in collaboration with *Die Yunge Yiddishe Kummer*, Gottlieb, Else Latzmann, Josade, and Gluck.

"David Umru was phlegmatic, thoughtful, and calm; that's why I'm inclined to say that he didn't have the typical Jewish temperament. He had a round face, thick lips, and a speech defect, but all that disappeared when he began to speak in public. When Peretz came to Kovno, it was David who introduced him to the audience. He always spoke without notes; he was very clear and precise. His exceptional intelligence was unmistakable to everyone who listened to him attentively. He was soft-spoken, a man of few words, who didn't waste his time in idle conversation. He was not talkative, but cautious and taciturn.

"He painted scenery for the theater. Although he followed the avant-garde movement, he liked realism, and his taste in colors had been influenced by Impressionism.

"His wife was a quiet person. It would quickly become obvious that she was very much in love with him. She never applauded, but she had a way of looking at him…

"His works didn't often have happy endings."

To go to the end of my quest is to go to Ponary, now Paneriai. In Ponary – a holiday resort town nestled in a magnificent forest on the outskirts of Vilna – seventy thousand Jews were killed under unspeakable circumstances.

Since 1992, two memorials have been erected, one by Jews, and the other – Paneriu memorialis – by Lithuanians. Here is

Butrimonys, 1936. Back row: Liuba Suganas, her brother, Benjamin Liackovitch, an unidentified man. Front row (also left to right): Liuba's son, Wolf Louis Suganas, her daughter, Solange Suganas, and an unidentified child.

the inscription that remained on the second, in Russian and in Lithuanian, until late 1990:

> *Here in the forests of Paneriai, from July 1941 to July 1944,*
> *Hitler's men killed more than one hundred thousand*
> *Soviet citizens. From December 1943 on, in order to hide*
> *all traces of their crimes, the Fascist forces occupying*
> *Lithuania burnt the bodies of their victims.*

A railroad track lies nearby; trains break the silence as they thundered past. Did Umru meet his death here? Benjamin, his brother and my uncle, is convinced that he did.

Birds have no borders; nothing – and everything – belongs to them.

Odile Suganas

The day of my departure is here. Lithuanian friends have come to drive me to the airport. We stop on the hill overlooking Vilna, and I gaze at all the steeples. Photos. We get back into the car.

"Will you come back to Lithuania?"

"I will. There is still so much I want to see and learn..."

The airport is crowded. One last look at my Lithuanian friends. Aliciya's eyes are glistening with tears.

On the plane. I shall go back to Vilna, of course. My grandparents are there. I can't forsake them. But next time I'll bring some tools to tidy up their tombs, and a vase for flowers.

Birds have no borders; nothing – and everything – belongs to them.

– Paris 1993

The restored grave of Sonia and Jacob Katz's son. The folded hands pictured on the gravestone mark his membership in the Cohen tribe. Standing: Daraustas, the young son of film producer Aliciya Zukauskaite and director Saulius Berzinis. (Courtesy of Philo Bregstein.)

Catharsis

You never get over your childhood. You think you have left it far behind, but it clings to you, piercing you to the core, adhering to your soul. One day, it shatters into pieces that get stuck right there, in your heart. An uneasy feeling that weighs you down, a feeling you reluctantly have to live with: something gnawing at you, as much physically as emotionally.

Intolerable.

Later in my life, some incident, trivial on the surface, but a rift widening into a chasm underneath; the fleeting image of a face, a gaze, suddenly would burst into me.

Without my being fully aware of it, some kind of a truth is beginning to emerge; I have trouble grasping its importance. The story begins, developing on its own, going forward and backward like threads unconsciously tied and untied.

Day after day, month after month, year after year, a skein is unraveling. Something obvious, so obvious as to be almost incredible, I thought later. The truth, though. Meanwhile, it was something that felt like a deep hollow, a yearning...something missing.

I had instinctively recreated the scents of the hearth. Blazes dying down into glowing embers, stealthily purring away. Moments full of grace spent staring at the flames in order to recapture what my life had been like at the farm where I lived as a child, immersed in a wonderful, natural world of vegetable smells and tastes.

The shock of coming back home, a home that meant nothing to me because I had never lived there; worse still, coming back was synonymous with total darkness.

Many years later, when I was to all appearances an adult, the beginning of summer, the whole summer actually, would become distressing – an unbearable season, a time when I could not breathe freely, a lead weight, a slow, heavy death. As emergency remedies, the sea and the countryside were the only places where I could get back on my feet again.

Once, during a winter holiday in Switzerland, while I was feeling very low, I happened to walk into a shop where fine handicraft was on display.
  Behind the counter, the face of an old woman stirred up a flood of feelings within me. Her immaculate, white skin was lightly furrowed by a few wrinkles, and her face, framed with white hair coiled up into a knot, was lit by blue, iris-like, softly gleaming eyes. Such charming old ladies were no longer found in cities, which made her all the more precious to me. The sight of her triggered a rush of emotion that filled my eyes. I dashed outside and started to walk on the snow-covered ground, trying to repress the wild sobs that made me tremble all over. Why did the sight of that old lady upset me so much? Why was I overwhelmed by this unexpected flood of tears? I couldn't understand it at all.

An uneasy feeling gripped my heart, an ache. I tried to figure it out.

That evening, in my room in the hotel in Kandersteg, I began to think back of Mirande, this little village in south west of France. Since I had left there, everything had gone wrong. A childhood ailment that had inexplicably lingered.

That is how I set out on a labyrinthine journey aimed at deciphering the sores and bruises on a little girl's heart.

I could not foresee then that I would be drawn back to the East.

The next day, like a print being developed, the first image that came to my mind was of Grandma Lacave's tall, lean figure. Elated, transfigured, I walked about the village as if I had hit the jackpot.

I left Kandersteg feeling as if it were an island at the end of the earth, a place that had offered me a revelation.

Grandma Lacave was synonymous with the war. Marie Lacave also coincided with the discovery of a new, peaceful world. Stability, simplicity, FREEDOM.

I had lived with her for three years.

Since the end of the war I had seen her only once. I was eleven then, and suffering from a terrible toothache that had canceled out any reaction to the visit. We corresponded for a long time; I have carefully kept her letters in the drawer of my bedside table.

Birds have no borders; nothing – and everything – belongs to them.

Once the war was over, everyone went back home. We drove up north. My world had collapsed.

Why had we had to leave Mirande?

I could not understand why we had broken away from a world in which I had been so content – happy without knowing it. Blissful, actually. Noisy processions of vehicles were moving to and fro. Later, I remembered only the endless line of army trucks driving south and the smell of gasoline. The crammed Peugeot was overloaded with boxes and bags.

Returning to the family home, our ultimate destination, was such a shock that I can only conjure up an impression of darkness and desolation when I try to remember our arrival in Rouen. The house had been vandalized and flooded.

My home, my real home, was the farm where I had been living free, in a world full of animals and lovely smells, among sturdy people. A warm, unpretentious family, a home from which I drew the strength that has sustained me until this very day.

A few weeks after Kandersteg, obeying an irresistible impulse, I decided to visit Mirande in the summer. I telephoned Paulette, one of Grandma Lacave's daughters, who also lived on a farm, to make sure she would be home.

A couple of days before leaving, I was strongly affected by a dream: My mother and I were trapped in a hole from which we eventually managed to escape. This dream proved to correspond to a past reality, as reported to me by Henriette, Grandma Lacave's elder daughter, that whenever they thought we were in danger they would take us down to hide, into a kind of improvised cellar. It had recently been sealed. How phenomenal was the strength of the subconscious as appeared the image of the stagnant pond where ducks used to swim.

The Gers region is not very far from the Landes where my parents had their summer house. I set out early in the morning.

I could not understand how I had managed to live up till then without going back. Every human being has an inner stock of magic words: Mirande was one of mine. Driving the old Renault, I set out on a trip of about one hundred twenty-five miles. An adventure dictated by my heart that had almost submerged my consciousness.

The monotonous green roads of the Landes with their dense mass of sandy forests were stretching away in the direction of the Gers.

There was a sharp contrast between the Landes and the Gascony countryside. The flat country of the Landes gave place to rolling hills glaring under the July sun, a landscape embroidered with vineyards and dotted with large, ancient, stone houses that gave me a feeling of eternity. I drove past a succession of fields, meadows, and villages, nicely flowered, that all seemed to beam at me.

A man-made landscape.

Overlooking the Gers river valley, I caught a glimpse, in distant profile, of the cathedral around which the town of Auch was clustered in a graceful display. The cathedral stood near the convent where many Jewish children had found shelter. More particularly, it was the place where my sister had been hidden, safe from human madness. Many years later, she told me that the nuns had kept her from joining the other boarders on their way to confession.

For all these reasons, Auch has a special place in my heart.

I treasure the recollection of the first and only visit I paid my sister at the convent. My mother and I had come by train. I have a clear memory of walking up a flight of impressive-looking stone steps. The Mother Superior, in a winged coif, standing at the top of the stairs, handed me – wonder of wonders! – a piece of candy. A taste I have never forgotten. I felt as if I had met God.

There is also an anecdote I have heard over and over about the time I ran away from home and my parents were in a panic. When we arrived in Mirande, my father had rented the first place he could find, a small, second-floor room across from the railway station. My parents started looking for me, expecting the worst. I was found sitting quietly in a carriage on a siding.

When asked what I was doing there, I said I was on my way to set my sister free, because she was unhappy in her convent. I myself have no recollection of this incident.

Later, I would often slip away from home and visit some old ladies who lived nearby. My parents no longer looked for me. They knew more or less where to find me.

Auch stands in my life story as an inescapable landmark along an initiatory path. I admired the elegant, massive, stone houses erected along Marne Avenue and Alsace Avenue, streets leading to the Holy Mary Cathedral. North of the cathedral there is a maze of *Pousterles*, a network of lanes connected by steps, dating from the Middle Ages. They looked familiar to me.

The author's family's first home in Mirande, across from the station. In front of the oleander, left to right: Wolf Louis, Solange, and Odile Suganas.

Before driving on to Mirande, I stopped at the cathedral, with its fine Renaissance façade. I wanted to revisit the wonderful stalls wrought from oak, with their elaborate, flamboyant carvings, thousands of easily identifiable biblical characters from the Old and the New Testaments, alternating male and female figures placed opposite each other.

With a thrill of pleasure I walked into the cathedral.

In a small chapel, I burned a candle for my sister.

Mirande. Odile in the courtyard in the first hiding place with the neighbor's dog, Sirène.

When I walked out, the sky was flooded with a clear, luminous, bright and blue light, a splendid introduction to Mirande.

I did not feel like seeing anything else in town.

I was about twelve miles away from Mirande. I drove on at a leisurely pace so I could enjoy the bright vegetation encroaching upon a serene sky, as in a blue and green painting.

In the distance, the cackling of the geese immediately took me back, as if by magic, to the country of my childhood.

For the first time in a very long time, indelible recollections from deep within me rose up, fresh and strong. Just as I had done years before, I listened to them, enraptured.

Sheer delight.

A signpost. Mirande. I drive to the center of the village, up to the Place d'Astarac, with its bandstand, unchanged in the square empty of people because of the summer heat. Over there, around the corner, stands the cafe where I cast the scene I had always

In the center, the farmhouse where the author and her mother were hidden.

pictured, as my mother had told me; it happened in 1942. A man walked up to her and asked if she was Mrs. Suganas.

"Why?" she hastily replied.

"Because I can tell you where your husband is."

Sitting there with her three children, holding me on her lap, with her blue eyes and fair hair, she was easy to identify.

That is how our life in Mirande began.

For safety reasons, my father did not live in the small apartment he had managed to rent. His technique in matters of security consisted of scattering the members of the family. One could never be too careful, in case there should be a police raid or a denunciation. He did not intend to let his wife and daughter stay there long, because the apartment had only one exit. For him, a back door was essential. That is what had saved him when the French police had come to his home in Rouen. In the meantime, before more suitable lodgings could be found, he fastened a rope to the window rail so that we could escape quickly in an emergency.

Restless and full of energy, my father had noticed that the Lacaves' farmhouse was located in a lonely spot. Although he did not know them, he took the risk of inquiring whether they would agree to keep, for his wife and child, the cow he had just bought, and they did. He then asked if they were willing to take in his wife and baby as well, with the difference that they were Jewish. That detail did not change anything in Marie and Gaston Lacave's decision. There was an understanding: the morning milk was for us, while the evening milk belonged to the farm. That is how I began to live in close contact with nature, according to the sun and the seasons. A way of life that was going to permeate all the cells of my being.

Mirande is where I was taught how to rub crusts of bread with garlic, to eat newly laid eggs by making a hole in them with a needle; and then there were the wonderful, huge slices of bread that I would spread with goose fat in some dark corner of the farm, dipping into one of the numerous earthen jars around. Ah! Goose fat and its unmistakable odor! I recently attended a luncheon party given by one of my colleagues to celebrate the birth of her son. When she set a huge dish of *confit d'oie* on the table, the scent of the fat caught me off guard, and I burst into tears in front of a dozen staring, nonplused guests. Embarrassed, I made up the first excuse that came to my mind to account for the outburst.

Then there was Jeannette, the goose-girl. I would go along with her although I was afraid of getting nipped.
Everything was discovery and adventure.
Now I understand. I felt free in the sun with green grass, good smells, animals, the sky, and my grandma around.

Grandma Lacave's farmhouse. The room the author shared with her mother is on the first floor on the left.

I also remember the barn, with its own particular smells, where tiny insects kept busy, where I could loll about far away from the world, where I could hop from one bundle of hay to the other. Pure fun!

Several other scenes are also rooted deep in my mind, happy recollections in warm-tinted flashes: the grape-gathering, and the path running down below, where I would stand, watching the whole operation. The vines looked tall to me, so very tall... The harvesters would pour out their full baskets into huge barrels set on horse carts. During those days I was mostly impressed by the dazzling brightness of the sun, spreading a mellow, gold tint of the autumn sunlight, the vine-leaves turning from yellow to russet, the noiseless labor of all and sundry, the harmony of the harvesters at one with nature. And the serenity emanating from it all.

That is what I received and tasted as a child, between the ages of two and five, a gift from nature that will remain in me as a well-kept secret until I die.

Happiness.

As for people, I have few recollections: My father singing to me; my sister wearing braids and arriving at the farm for the holidays, sitting on the luggage rack of Mr. Riou's bicycle; Jeannette and her geese. None of my mother, perhaps because she was part of myself; but I do remember Marie Lacave's constant presence, as she stood in the farmyard, a very thin, tall, dignified, severe-looking woman, always wearing black. To me she looked very old; actually, she was not yet forty. I recall no demonstrative marks of affection, but I had only to look around and she was there, always the same. She remains an everlasting image in my inner vision and so does the fragrant smell of the hearth around which she would busy herself in the evening.

For me, Mirande – or, more precisely, Valentès, the name of the place where the farm stood – meant peace. There, I heard bird songs for the first time – the nightingale, harbinger of spring; the call for the renewal of life.

These musical awakenings remain forever engraved in my heart.

Valentès. Marie and Gaston Lacave in front of their farmhouse.

Leaving Mirande was the worst thing that could have happened to me. My wings were clipped.

Nothing was said or explained. I can't even remember the day we left.

The world of adults is utterly unfair and impossible to understand.

Much later, incidentally, I learned that Grandma Lacave had passed away in 1972; having missed something important I felt I should have known made me feel overdrawn by the events.

But time, like an animal lying in wait, was on the lookout, holding out for an auspicious moment...

Mirande became a painful yearning, a permanent weariness.

But of that, too, it took me a long time to become aware.

January 5, 1997. In the mail, a letter from Yad Vashem, Jerusalem.

I had forgotten.

It had been four years since I had sent in the application. I was informed by a short letter that the certificate of the Righteous Among the Nations (awarded by Yad Vashem to people who saved Jews during the war) was going to be given to Marie and Gaston Lacave, with their four children accepting it in their name.

The ceremony was to take place on the 30th of the same month at the town hall in Mirande.

Speechless at first, then beside myself with joy, I picked up the phone and called Mother to let her know the big news. "Well deserved!" she said. "I am so glad." Two causes for rejoicing: the award itself, and the opportunity to go back to Mirande.

From that day on, I thought of nothing else.

Odile Suganas

I called Henriette in Mirande. They, too, had received the letter, and wanted a quiet, private ceremony.

January 30, 1997. The Paris-Toulouse plane. Henriette and I have planned to meet at the station in Auch. Because of a strike, the station is deserted. I am early and have plenty of time to read the commemorative plaque.

The first trainload of conscripts from the Gers region who were sent to forced labor camps in nazi Germany left the railway station in Auch on Wednesday, March 13, 1943.

The United, Interdependent, Faithful Survivors

LET US NEVER FORGET.

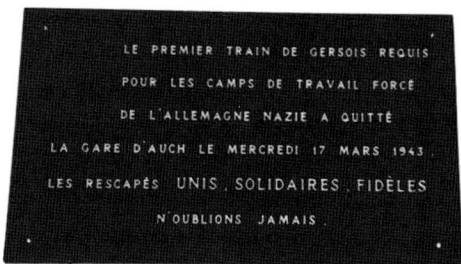

Plaque on the station wall in Auch.

Two chestnut trees mark out the square on each side. It is almost lunchtime; the quiet square is bustling with people on their way home. After waiting about twenty minutes, I see Henriette's car pulling up with her daughter-in-law, Annie-Christine, at the wheel. Of the four children, Henriette is the one who looks most like Marie Lacave. She has the same style, the same friendly smile. Annie-Christine is a straightforward, lively young woman. We immediately feel at ease with one another, and I take special pleasure in the singing grace of their matchless accent – sunshine in the middle of winter.

At lunch at Henriette's, we meet her son, Jean-Michel, and her brother, Léon. We are all somewhat agitated. The ceremony is to take place very shortly.

From left to right: Paulette Lacave's daughter, Marie-Claude Lacave; Léon Lacave; Odile Suganas; Paulette Lacave Lapèze; Paulette's husband, Albert Lapèze.

I went back to Mirande for the first time in the early nineteen-fifties.

My second visit, after Kandersteg, took place on a hot day in the middle of August. After lunch we repaired to Paulette's farm down the hill from her parents' home. Her farm was a busy place filled with geese, pigs, hens, ducks, turkeys, and cows. Paulette, her husband, and their daughter, Marie-Claude, were waiting for me. As a matter of course, as if it were an everyday present, Paulette handed me some fragrant confit. They did not ask why I had come. They pointed through the window to the top of the hill, to a dark spot in the distance, Marie and Gaston's farm. Despite the summer heat, I was impatient to get up there; they must have wondered why a grown woman should be so attached to that house. Henriette joined us at the farm.

Emile and Léon, who had both remained single, had recently moved out of the house, but nothing had changed; it remained as it used to be. As soon as we got there, I recognized the layout. It was a fine farmhouse with large rooms, all similarly shaped, each opening onto the ancient flagstone entrance hall, at the far end of which a wide staircase led to the first floor. What a fine building it was!

At the heart of the house – kitchen, dining room, and living room rolled into one – an immense fireplace stood, with two benches inside. The patina laid by time had given it a splendid gloss. NOTHING had changed, not even the small, Vichy, blue-checked curtain hanging above the fireplace, faded stiff with forty years of dust. It seemed that everything had happened just yesterday; time no longer existed. Sleeping Beauty's house.

But time had rolled on. Paulette, Emile, Léon, and Henriette stood by, moved. For them, the conjuring up of the past had revived a happy, peaceful family life, now over. No questions were raised; there was no need for it. And for me, their warm welcome spoke for itself. For all of us, being together was enough. Although,

The farm at Valentès; Grandma Lacave's fireplace.

later, as we were standing apart, Henriette asked me, in a tone of curiosity tinged with concern, "Why were you so eager to see the farm again?" And after a moment's hesitation, she looked at me with questioning eyes: "Does it mean that much to you? You were so young…" It puzzled her, but through insight, sensitivity, and intelligence, she had guessed that somewhere there was a thread holding my story together.

She immediately understood that she had struck home.

I made a promise. "I will explain everything one day, when we have a little time."

I remember that, on the third trip to Mirande, with my parents and my sister, my father was beside himself with joy; he insisted on going everywhere. He had never been partial to walking, but that day, handling his walking-stick like a general leading his troops, he ordered us in a peremptory voice to hurry, so impatient was he to see the village again. Suddenly turning voluble, he began mentioning people and events, pointing with his stick to the places where a part of his life story had taken place.

I understood only much later, after he had passed away, that the village brought him back to the world he had come from, to the shtetl where he had been born.

We walked across the small municipal gardens to the town hall: an elegant, attractive building in the Second Empire style. Low steps led to the entrance hall. We were ushered into the reception room. After a few minutes, the mayor, the vice prefect, the Israeli consul, and the representative of Yad Vashem in France made their entrance. After the introductions, each of them made a heartfelt speech revealing the interest they had taken in the Lacave family, both personally, and as a significant part of History. Henriette betrayed her emotion; Paulette stealthily wiped her eyes; Léon's smile melted into tears. The Israeli consul told how my father had met the Lacaves thanks to a cow, and everyone laughed, lightening the atmosphere.

Calling up these memories was all the more valuable and impactful on this very special day. I said a few words. "A man dies twice: the first time, when he passes away; the second time, when everyone has forgotten him. That will not happen to Marie and Gaston Lacave."

Congratulations. Henriette and Paulette were offered champagne and flowers. Photos were taken. I received a beautiful book about Mirande, inscribed by the mayor.

Mirande, January 30, 1997; award ceremony at the Town Hall. From left to right: Léon Lacave; Paulette Lacave Lapèze; Lucien Fayman from the French Committee for Yad Vashem; Anita Mazor, the Israeli consul in Marseille; Pierre Baudran, mayor of Mirande; Gérard Gavory, sous-préfet; far right (mostly cut off), Henriette Lacave Loumagne.

Lost in thought, we returned home in silence, our arms full of flowers.

In the afternoon, with Henriette and Léon, we visited the tiny churchyard in Valentès where Marie and Gaston Lacave were buried. The place was peaceful, just as I had found it so many years before: neat and tidy, carefully tended.

Once again I read:
"Marie Lacave 1899-1972 and Gaston Lacave 1891-1968."

The silk roses in the basket I set down on the grave made a spot of color on the white slab of their tombstone. Henriette left some of the flowers she had been given, and Léon, probably out of habit, pretended to remove some weeds that were not there.

Odile Suganas

Saint-Paul-les-Dax, 1997; the Lacaves on a visit to Liuba Suganas's home. Seated, from left to right: Léon Lacave, Liuba Suganas, Henriette Lacave Loumagne. Standing, from left to right: Liuba's grandson, Laurent Solomon; Odile Suganas; Annie-Christine Loumagne, Henriette's daughter-in-law; Jean-Michel Loumagne.

I had reached the end of my journey; I had come full circle.

– Paris, February 1999

Genealogy

A family tree: my mother's line

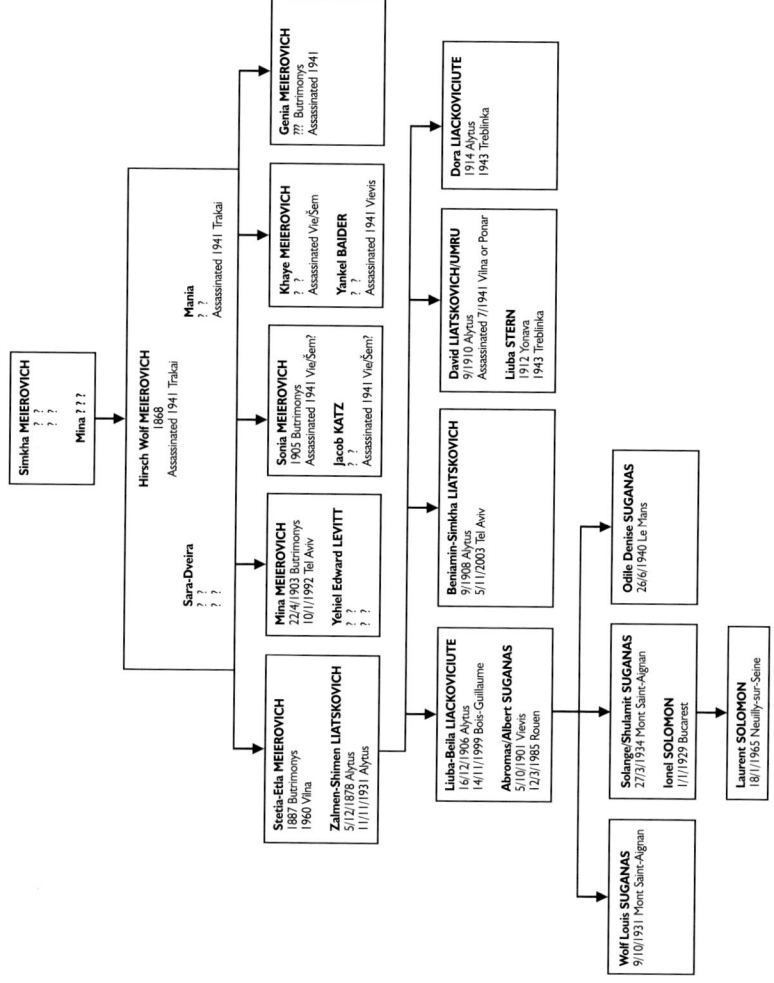

A family tree: my father's line

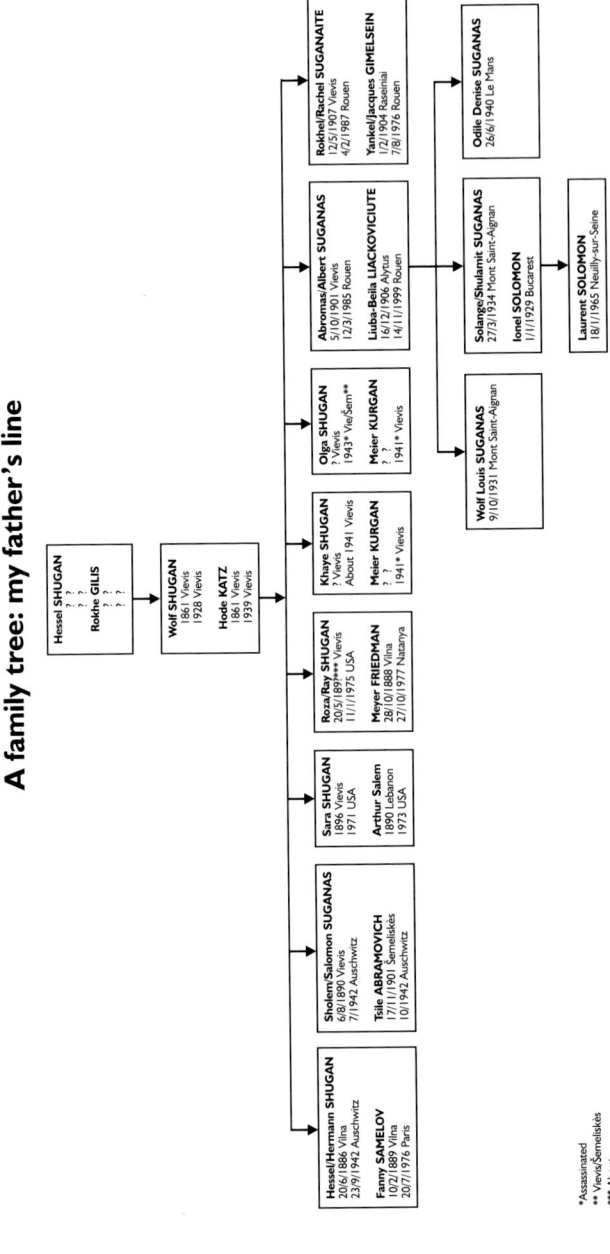

*Assassinated
*** Vievis/Šemeliškės
*** About